100 DAYS TO A STOIC MIND

100 DAYS TO A STOIC MIND. Copyright © 2024 by St. Martin's Press.
All rights reserved. Printed in the United States of America. For information, address
St. Martin's Publishing Group, 120 Broadway, New York, NY 10271.

www.castlepointbooks.com

The Castle Point Books trademark is owned by Castle Point Publishing, LLC.
Castle Point books are published and distributed by St. Martin's Publishing Group.

ISBN 978-1-250-35881-3 (paper over board)
ISBN 978-1-250-35882-0 (ebook)

Cover design by Tara Long
Interior design by Joanna Williams
Editorial by Monica Sweeney
Images used under license by Shutterstock.com

All quotations, unless otherwise noted, are taken or adapted from the following sources:

A Selection from the Discourses of Epictetus with the Encheiridion by Epictetus
and translated by George Long.

Discourses by Epictetus.

Meditations by Marcus Aurelius Antoninus.

Seneca's Letters from a Stoic by Lucius Annaeus Seneca.

Seneca's Morals of a Happy Life, Benefits, Anger and Clemency by Lucius Annaeus Seneca.

Our books may be purchased in bulk for promotional, educational, or business use. Please
contact your local bookseller or the Macmillan Corporate and Premium Sales Department at
1-800-221-7945, extension 5442, or by email at MacmillanSpecialMarkets@macmillan.com.

First Edition: 2024

10 9 8 7 6 5 4 3 2 1

100 DAYS TO A STOIC MIND

BRYAN SENA

CASTLE POINT BOOKS

NEW YORK

THE PATH TO A STOIC MIND

One hundred days. What if you promised to run ten miles every morning for the next hundred days? You'd quit before you started. What if you swore to give up your big vice for nearly a quarter of the year? You might find a cheat day sooner than later. One hundred days is a lot if you're attempting to make a seismic change. But what if you made a disciplined approach to changing your life by reading one idea a day and allowing your mindset to shift? Then one hundred days is nothing.

In one hundred days, you can tap into and harness the Stoic mind. Not "stoic," like the way the word is used today to mean moody and dead-eyed. But someone who is in control, who sees opportunity in the struggle, and who can be the calm in a storm. Take the Stoics themselves. The philosophers who chose reason and self-control over chaos and weakness. Over half a millennium, they collected and honed values that identified the path to the highest good.

It started in ancient Greece with Zeno of Citium in Athens during the third century BCE, then great thinkers of all walks of life took these foundations and built something sturdy and true. From Cato the Younger and Seneca to Epictetus and Marcus Aurelius—among them statesmen, an enslaved man turned teacher, and one of the most respected emperors of ancient Rome—these founders of Stoicism left clear guidelines for how to achieve happiness and tranquility through self-control, resilience, humility, and levelheadedness.

FOUR VALUES DEFINE A STOIC MIND. THEY ARE COURAGE, TEMPERANCE, JUSTICE, AND WISDOM.

Courage is doing the right thing even when it's hard, powering through the pain, and finding an opportunity, a lesson, or a new door despite adversity. It's staring fear in the face and seeing an unworthy opponent.

Temperance is balance, moderation, and discipline. It's keeping your vices and impulses in check and staying the course with what's good and logical.

Justice is fairness, moral integrity, and looking out for the group and not the individual. It's knowing that at the end of the day, human beings have more in common than not.

Wisdom is humility, strength, and knowledge with a bird's-eye view. It's keeping it together and knowing what's in your control, what isn't, and how to react accordingly.

Any practitioner of Stoicism will tell you never to bite off more than you can chew. In *100 Days to a Stoic Mind*, very little will be asked of you and yet you will earn a high reward. Read one line a day from one of the great Stoics and consider its meaning. You'll be presented with a task, a reflection, a journaling prompt, or a tool that will help you through challenges as you learn to adopt a Stoic mindset. Occasionally you'll be given a snapshot into the lives of other Stoics, from the founders to modern thinkers. In the time it takes you to drink a few sips of your morning beverage, you'll have the spark of inspiration you need to build a road map to a life of satisfaction, resilience, and tranquility.

"FIRE TESTS GOLD AND ADVERSITY TESTS THE BRAVE."

—Seneca, *Minor Dialogues*

TODAY'S STOIC READING

Minor Dialogues, 1.5.17
—SENECA

THE STRUGGLE IS THE WAY.

Everyone is tested, but the best face it head-on. Where others crumble from misfortune, you find a lesson, a skill, a new way forward. Gold shows its strength when met with fire.

STOIC EXERCISE ●

Cold Plunge: 30 seconds. Practice endurance in the face of adversity through cold water therapy. Fill a bathtub with cold water and ice. In this context, easing in will make it worse—just get right in. Endure the discomfort for thirty seconds. Begin to train your mind to access its resilience.

"NO MAN IS FREE WHO IS NOT MASTER OF HIMSELF."

—Epictetus, *Discourses*

FREEDOM IS FOUND WITHIN.

You cannot control everything, but you can control your thoughts and reactions. Resist being driven by outside influences, like status, consumerism, and other people's behavior. You are the driver, and you can choose how to navigate your path.

STOIC EXERCISE ●

Discipline Check: Practice restraint today. When tested, resist responding with fire. Write down the heated emotion and return to it with a cool reflection.

"THAT WHICH IS NOT GOOD FOR THE SWARM, NEITHER IS IT GOOD FOR THE BEE."

—Marcus Aurelius, *Meditations*

TODAY'S STOIC READING

Meditations, 6.54
—Marcus Aurelius

A BENEFIT TO OTHERS IS A BENEFIT TO YOU.

Acting in self-interest has short-term gains. A hive functions as a collective, and it always yields results when everyone does their part. When they don't, the hive cannot survive. Focus on how your impact helps your team, your family, your friends, and your circles.

STOIC EXERCISE ●

Gratitude: Make a list of five ways your circle has supported you.

AN EYE ON THE PHILOSOPHER

Marcus Aurelius (121–180 CE), also known as Marcus Aurelius Antoninus, was a Roman emperor and Stoic philosopher. His philosophy: cultivate inner peace through self-discipline, embrace the present moment, and accept the natural course of events with equanimity.

"WASTE NO MORE TIME ARGUING ABOUT WHAT A GOOD MAN SHOULD BE. BE ONE."

—Marcus Aurelius, *Meditations*

LESS TALKING, MORE DOING.

Be the person you say you are. Show up, be present, and never expect more from others than you can manage yourself. Keep an even keel while being tenaciously focused on doing the right thing. Talking is preparation, but action is success.

STOIC EXERCISE ●

Think on your principles. What makes a good person? What traits do you have or aspire to achieve that honor this idea?

"IT IS NOT DEATH THAT A MAN SHOULD FEAR, BUT HE SHOULD FEAR NEVER BEGINNING TO LIVE."

—Marcus Aurelius, *Meditations*

FOCUS ON LIVING.

No matter who you are, where you come from, or however highly you think of yourself, none of us gets out alive. Stop wasting time fearing death. Live fully and treat life as a journey.

STOIC EXERCISE ●

Compel yourself to imagine a life worth living. List the good and bad aspects of something you have been wanting to do but are worried won't work out. Which list is longer?

"IF YOU SEEK TRANQUILITY, DO LESS."

—Marcus Aurelius, *Meditations*

WORK SMARTER, NOT HARDER.

Looking busy is the great lie. Giving yourself more to do than you need, splashing around just to make waves, and creating work where there is none will not move you forward or bring you ease. Stick to what's essential.

STOIC EXERCISE ●

Collect Stoic practices like marbles. Feel them turn in your hands, considering which insight will bring you guidance at that moment. A Stoic knows not to get overwhelmed by inflated axioms and instead chooses the simplest, logic-driven answer.

"TREAT YOUR INFERIORS AS YOU WOULD BE TREATED BY YOUR BETTERS."

—Seneca, *Moral Letters to Lucilius*

| | TODAY'S STOIC READING |

Moral Letters to Lucilius, 47.11
—SENECA

ABIDE BY THE GOLDEN RULE.

Treat others with the respect and humanity you wish for yourself.

Finding pleasure in another's misfortune is not the power bank to your success, but a drain on your battery. Embody reason and fairness in all things.

STOIC EXERCISE ●

Journal Reflection: From Roman emperors to modern presidents, the great Stoics share a throughline in their practice. Letter writing and journaling—the penned thoughts that would stand the test of time— are critical building blocks for modern Stoics. Keep it simple. Track what you see each day and take note of your reactions.

"FOLLOW EVERY MAN WHO IS STRONGER THAN YOURSELF."

—Epictetus, *Discourses*

| TODAY'S STOIC READING
Discourses, 2.13
—EPICTETUS

KNOW WHEN TO LET OTHERS LEAD.

Someone else's strength isn't a threat, it's an asset. Follow it, learn it, emulate it. Don't let petty insecurity prevent you from recognizing vitality in others. Let it make you better.

STOIC EXERCISE ●

Do Hard Things: Use a stopwatch to time yourself holding a forearm plank for as long as you can. When you start to tire, push harder. Keep your mind focused on a strength you want to build, be it physical or mental. Visualize your success.

THE STOIC TRANSLATOR

Impatient Mind: "I want immediate results. Waiting and working patiently is too frustrating."

Stoic Mind: "Good things take time and effort. I'll practice patience and persistence, trusting the process and my ability to endure."

"THERE ARE MORE THINGS LIKELY TO FRIGHTEN US THAN THERE ARE TO CRUSH US."

—Seneca, *Moral Letters to Lucilius*

TODAY'S STOIC READING

Moral Letters to Lucilius, 13.4
—Seneca

FEAR IS AN ILLUSION.

Worry less. Fears of what someone thinks of you or the worst possible outcomes are distractions. Use your imagination for something greater than anxious trains of thought. Let this creativity propel you forward rather than hold you back.

STOIC EXERCISE ●

Make a list of five things you are afraid of. Which of these are within your control? What is the first step in dominating those fears?

"LIFE IS WELL ENOUGH FURNISHED, BUT WE ARE TOO GREEDY WITH REGARD TO ITS FURNISHINGS; SOMETHING ALWAYS SEEMS TO US LACKING, AND WILL ALWAYS SEEM LACKING."

—Seneca, *Moral Letters to Lucilius*

TODAY'S STOIC READING

Moral Letters to Lucilius, 61.4
—SENECA

BE GREEDY WITH NOTHING AND YOU WILL HAVE EVERYTHING.

Set your expectations to be grateful for what is. Maximalism will fill physical spaces, but it won't fill the voids in your mind and heart. To want more is to miss what's in front of you.

STOIC EXERCISE ●

Scholarly Pause: Spend thirty minutes reading about financial restriction, minimalism, or work-life balance. Approach your reading with the mindset that less is more.

"LIFE SHOULD NOT BE OUT OF HARMONY WITH...WORDS."

—Seneca, *Moral Letters to Lucilius*

TURN YOUR WORDS INTO VERBS.

Make promises to yourself and others that you can keep. Live your words as best you can, because failing at something you've tried is more valuable than never trying it at all.

STOIC EXERCISE ●

Consider a goal that feels like a tall order. Map out the first three steps toward making that goal a reality, regardless of how inconsequential they may seem.

"LET YOUR FAULTS DIE BEFORE YOU DIE."

—Seneca, *Moral Letters to Lucilius*

DAY	TODAY'S STOIC READING
12	*Moral Letters to Lucilius*, 27.2 —Seneca

AGE OUT OF YOUR VICES.

Don't keep carrying the baggage your younger self packed.

Be grateful for the journey but let go of the trivial wants and superficial desires that no longer serve your present self. Recognize what you need now and decide which priorities you should take with you on the road ahead.

STOIC EXERCISE ●

Discipline Check: Indite your indulgences. What vices did your younger self move mountains for that you no longer care about? Which ones are still kicking around?

"MEN WHO HIDE THEIR SINS CAN NEVER COUNT UPON REMAINING HIDDEN; FOR THEIR CONSCIENCE CONVICTS THEM AND REVEALS THEM TO THEMSELVES."

—Seneca, *Moral Letters to Lucilius*

TODAY'S STOIC READING

Moral Letters to Lucilius, 97.16
—SENECA

THE SKELETONS IN YOUR CLOSET WILL START KNOCKING.

Don't make later you responsible for cleaning up present you's mess.
You can try all you want to hide mistakes, dig ditches to bury your
wrongdoings, or rationalize faults so that you come out on top. When
you know something isn't right, get ahead of it now. Own your failures.

STOIC EXERCISE ●

Gratitude: When have you been grateful for losing? Consider five losses
or misses and how they impacted you for the better.

A MODERN SPOTLIGHT

Nelson Mandela The anti-apartheid revolutionary and first Black
president of South Africa exemplified Stoic pillars through his
enduring resilience despite spending twenty-seven years in prison.
The ethos? Embrace hardship with dignity, maintain control over your
emotions, and prioritize justice and harmony over personal vendettas.

"EVEN IF SOME OBSTACLE ARISES, IT IS BUT LIKE AN INTERVENING CLOUD, WHICH FLOATS BENEATH THE SUN BUT NEVER PREVAILS AGAINST IT."

—Seneca, *Moral Letters to Lucilius*

DAY 14 | TODAY'S STOIC READING

Moral Letters to Lucilius, 27.3
—Seneca

THIS TOO SHALL PASS.

Hurdles are meant to be surmounted. Don't confuse temporary obstacles with walls that are impossible to climb. Treat your worries and fleeting frustrations with the preparation and clarity with which you would approach a thunderstorm. It could be benign or brutal, but it will pass.

STOIC EXERCISE ●

Identify a symbol of strength. Like the sun in the quote above, what symbol is still standing when the clouds part? Return to this symbol—whether in your mind, with a fidget object, a photo on your phone, or even a tattoo or an art piece—when you need reminders of this symbol of resilience.

"NO SERVITUDE IS MORE DISGRACEFUL THAN THAT WHICH IS SELF-IMPOSED."

—Seneca, *Moral Letters to Lucilius*

DON'T TRAP YOURSELF IN A FALSE SENSE OF DUTY.

Reject the idea that perceived obligation and misguided loyalty should rule your choices. From feeding toxic relationships and sticking around in a job you hate to enduring what's bad for you inorder to avoid conflict, there is a difference between character-building struggle and foolish masochism. The latter serves no one.

STOIC EXERCISE ●

Meditation: 5 minutes. Find a quiet space. Sit upright in silence or with white noise, like the sound of a fan, rushing water, or the wind. Relax your body and let your palms rest on your knees. Let the traffic of your thoughts buzz and slowly disperse.

"VIRTUE ALONE AFFORDS EVERLASTING AND PEACE-GIVING JOY."

—Seneca, *Moral Letters to Lucilius*

TODAY'S STOIC READING

Moral Letters to Lucilius, 27.3
—Seneca

KEEP YOUR EYE ON THE PRIZE.

Integrity first. Don't get pulled away from your core principles. Enduring satisfaction and happiness come from remaining vigilant in your values and swatting away distractions that reduce your sense of self.

STOIC EXERCISE ●

What are signs of integrity? Come up with a list of five people who embody your idea of integrity and steadfastness in their values. They can be personal connections or famous people throughout history.

"IT DOES NOT MATTER WHAT YOU BEAR, BUT HOW YOU BEAR IT."

—Seneca, *Minor Dialogues*

RESILIENCE FAVORS THE BRAVE.

No one said the path would be easy, so train for endurance.

When a challenge is in front of you, don't let the intensity of the moment send you careening off the ledge. Know that the only way forward is through. Summon your grit and push forward.

STOIC EXERCISE

Cold Plunge: 1 minute. Endure the discomfort for a full minute and begin to train your mind to access its resilience.

AN EYE ON THE PHILOSOPHER

Zeno of Citium (c. 334–262 BCE) founded the Stoic school of philosophy in Athens. After a shipwreck led him to philosophy, he developed Stoicism's core teachings on virtue, wisdom, and living in harmony with nature. His pillars? Virtue is the only true good, and living according to nature leads to a fulfilled life.

"DOES ANY MAN THEN HINDER ME FROM GOING WITH SMILES AND CHEERFULNESS AND CONTENTMENT?"

—Epictetus, *Discourses*

YOUR ATTITUDE IS YOUR BUSINESS.

One person's influence can shift your mood only if you let them.

Access self-determination, define your happiness, and refuse to let intruders meddle with the tone you have set for yourself. Your contentment is defined by you and only you.

STOIC EXERCISE ●

When faced with negative emotions, do your worst on paper.

Get out the frustration and then rip up, discard, or burn the reflection. Let the disintegrated pieces of your feelings function as your catharsis.

THIS STOIC IN HISTORY

Abraham Lincoln The slavery-ending president had a trick in times of stress: writing "hot letters"—angry, unfiltered letters he never sent—to process his emotions and respond with calm rationality. Lincoln's lesson: control your reactions, focus on what you can change, and lead with wisdom and resilience in the face of turmoil.

"HOW CAN OUR PRINCIPLES BECOME DEAD, UNLESS THE IMPRESSIONS WHICH CORRESPOND TO THEM ARE EXTINGUISHED? BUT IT IS IN YOUR POWER CONTINUOUSLY TO FAN THESE THOUGHTS INTO A FLAME."

—Marcus Aurelius, *Meditations*

APATHY IS THE DEATH OF INTEGRITY.

Staying true to your principles isn't a passive game. Even if the things you care about come easily, don't let yourself feel entitled to what you know is right. Stay vigilant in your core beliefs, honor them, and defend them always.

STOIC EXERCISE ●

Journal Reflection: Map out your principles and reflect upon why they matter to you. Make a chart and connect the core value with the actions you perform to make those values have true meaning.

"OFFER THANKS
EITHER TO YOUR
GOOD LUCK OR
TO YOUR CAUTION…
HOWEVER,
CAUTION CAN
EFFECT NOTHING
BUT TO MAKE
YOU UNGENEROUS."

—Seneca, *Moral Letters to Lucilius*

TO WITHHOLD IS TO BE WITHOUT.

When you narrowly avoid a misfortune or an encounter with ungrateful people, it's tempting to decide that the avoidance itself is the key. But to scrupulously avoid or to be too precautionary is to miss opportunities entirely.

STOIC EXERCISE

Scholarly Pause: Dive deeper into your Stoic practice and read from an original Stoic text for thirty minutes. Become an active reader and take notes or mark up the lines that intrigue you.

"THEY WHISPER THE BASEST OF PRAYERS TO HEAVEN; BUT IF ANYONE LISTENS, THEY ARE SILENT AT ONCE."

—Seneca, *Moral Letters to Lucilius*

OWN WHO YOU ARE AT YOUR LOWEST POINT.

You will not always act in ways that will make you proud.

But you don't need to deny the existence of your struggles to maintain your self-worth. Consider what would happen if you recognized out loud what you'd ordinarily keep quiet.

STOIC EXERCISE ●

Do Hard Things: Make time for shadow work. Take accountability for your negative traits. Make a list of the qualities you do not admire about yourself and consider ways to turn them around.

"I HAVE LEARNED TO BE GENTLE AND MEEK, AND TO REFRAIN FROM ALL ANGER AND PASSION."

—Marcus Aurelius, *Meditations*

	TODAY'S STOIC READING
	Meditations, 1.1
	—MARCUS AURELIUS

TAKE IT DOWN A NOTCH.

Embrace the Zen. Strength is stepping away from ferocity, not toward it. Understand that gentleness is a willingness to look aggression in the face and feel a cool breeze instead of a storm. Let it blow on by.

STOIC EXERCISE ●

The next time you feel anger rising, take a moment to pause and breathe deeply. Visualize a calm and serene place. Commit to responding with gentleness and observe how it affects the situation and your inner state.

"REMEMBER THAT NOT ONLY THE DESIRE OF POWER AND RICHES MAKE US MEAN AND SUBJECT TO OTHERS."

—Epictetus, *Discourses*

CHECK YOUR VIRTUE.

Greed isn't the only vice that can lead you astray.

What have you made yourself a slave to? Decide if the goals you have set for yourself are principled, or if you are so laser-focused that you'll walk over others to get there.

STOIC EXERCISE ●

Gratitude: Appreciate the forest for the trees. What big-picture areas of your life do you have a healthy relationship with, whether it's free time, discipline, family, or something else?

THE STOIC TRANSLATOR

Anxious Mind: "I'm overwhelmed. I don't know how to handle it."
Stoic Mind: "I will focus on what I can control, break the problem into manageable parts, and approach it with calm determination."

"IT IS NOT THE MAN WHO HAS TOO LITTLE, BUT THE MAN WHO CRAVES MORE, THAT IS POOR."

—Seneca, *Moral Letters to Lucilius*

TODAY'S STOIC READING

Moral Letters to Lucilius, 2.6
—SENECA

YOUR THIRST IS ALREADY QUENCHED.

You have what you need. When you let competition and the desire for more, more, more cloud your vision, you lose sight of what really matters. Riches are all around you, but they're not in the form of money or things.

STOIC EXERCISE

Discipline Check: Scrutinize your excesses and ditch five of them. Choose any of five items or expenses that you know you do not need. Discard, delete, or donate them.

"THE BEST KIND OF REVENGE IS, NOT TO BECOME LIKE THEM."

—Marcus Aurelius, *Meditations*

TODAY'S STOIC READING

Meditations, 6.6
—MARCUS AURELIUS

REVENGE IS BEST SERVED BY SOMEONE ELSE.

Move on. Use the energy you would have put toward awaiting someone else's demise to detach yourself, not dig yourself a ditch alongside them. Stay true to you who are and don't let the gravitational pull of a negative situation suck you in.

STOIC EXERCISE ●

Breathwork: Breathwork helps reduce stress and clear your mind. Do a session of box breathing and consider adding it as a practice to your routine. Inhale evenly through your nose as you count to four. Pause, holding your breath to a count of four. Exhale evenly, again counting to four. Pause again, holding your breath to a count of four, then repeat the process.

"FIRST DIGEST THE THING, THEN DO NOT VOMIT IT UP."

—Epictetus, *Discourses*

THINK BEFORE YOU SPEAK.

Sit with new ideas and thoughts. Ruminate on the information and let it proliferate meaningful reflections in your mind. Speak only when you have something to say, and avoid spewing nonsense at all costs.

STOIC EXERCISE ●

Practice active listening. Make a point today to engage in at least one mindful conversation. Speak only with intention and remain silent otherwise in a conscious effort to let the other person navigate their thoughts without interruption.

"IF IT IS NOT RIGHT, DO NOT DO IT; IF IT IS NOT TRUE, DO NOT SAY IT."

—Marcus Aurelius, *Meditations*

PRACTICE INTEGRITY IN ALL ENDEAVORS.

It doesn't have to be that hard. Be truthful to yourself and to others. Measure your choices by whether they yield the ethical good. If they do not, then it is not the right choice.

STOIC EXERCISE ●

Do Hard Things: Commit to volunteer your time in a way that is inconvenient for you for the benefit of someone else. Chip in at a soup kitchen. Canvas for local politics. Tutor someone in your field. Talk to a stranger meaningfully.

A MODERN SPOTLIGHT

Maya Angelou The renowned poet, memoirist, and civil rights activist exemplified Stoic principles through her resilience, wisdom, and unwavering sense of self. Angelou's vision: "You may not control all the events that happen to you, but you can decide not to be reduced by them," reflecting the Stoic idea of maintaining inner strength and dignity in the face of adversity.

"A MAN IS SHELTERED JUST AS WELL BY A THATCH AS BY A ROOF OF GOLD."

—Seneca, *Moral Letters to Lucilius*

YOUR NEEDS ARE MET IN SIMPLICITY.

Set status aside. Money can only get you so far, but where does fulfillment actually reside? Observe what you actually need and take stock of what it offers you.

STOIC EXERCISE ●

Journal Reflection: Continue your journaling practice with these questions: What do you need? What do you have that you thought you needed, but in truth, is superfluous? Consider what you are grateful for having that isn't ostentatious.

"WHY FEAR THOSE WHO WRONGLY CENSURE YOU?"

—Epictetus, *The Echiridion*

TODAY'S STOIC READING

The Echiridion, 35
—EPICTETUS

UNJUST CRITICISMS ARE JUST NOISE.

Haters always find a way to spout their nonsense. You have
nothing to fear if you know what's true. Don't shrink into a corner
at the first criticism, but remind yourself of the central veracity,
the core of your principles.

STOIC EXERCISE ●

Meditation: 10 minutes. Find a quiet space. Sit upright in silence or with
white noise like the sound of a fan, rushing water, or the wind. Relax your
body and let your palms rest on your knees. Imagine stress floating away
as if on a gust of wind.

"DESPISE EVERYTHING THAT USELESS TOIL CREATES AS AN ORNAMENT AND AN OBJECT OF BEAUTY."

—Seneca, *Moral Letters to Lucilius*

SUPERFICIALITY SERVES NO ONE.

Resist the urge to let commercialism and meaningless objects rule your motivations. Working tirelessly toward a shallow sense of success will take more from you than it gives.

STOIC EXERCISE ●

Half the battle against materialism is resisting the point between when you decide you want something and taking it. Make impulse control your mantra. When you feel the urge to buy something, wait twenty-four hours before making the purchase.

"TAKE AWAY THE COMPLAINT... AND THE HARM IS TAKEN AWAY."

—Marcus Aurelius, *Meditations*

	TODAY'S STOIC READING
	Meditations, 4.7
	—MARCUS AURELIUS

STEP AWAY AND FIND PEACE.

Not all problems are worthy adversaries. Your complaint may feel righteous in the moment, but if you step aside and let it move past you, has it really harmed you at all? If you dismiss the idea that something is a problem, you may find that you are right.

STOIC EXERCISE ●

Scholarly Pause: Read or listen to a text written by a Stoic or a Stoicism admirer for thirty minutes. Remove any outside distractions and be fully present.

"WHY DO YOU UNDERTAKE A THING THAT IS IN NO WAY FIT FOR YOU? LEAVE IT TO THOSE WHO ARE ABLE TO DO IT, AND TO DO IT WELL."

—Epictetus, *Discourses*

TODAY'S STOIC READING

Discourses, 3.21
—Epictetus

NOT ALL GLORY IS MEANT FOR YOU.

Know your limits, know your strengths, and don't confuse the two.
Rather than taking on tasks that would be better run across the finish line by someone more fit to do it, let them. Be humble in knowing that not everything is meant for you, because something else is.

STOIC EXERCISE ●

Discipline Check: Cut your losses. What do you need to identify as wasted energy? Adjust your viewfinder and decide what pursuit would be a better use of your time.

"LOOK ABOUT YOU FOR THE OPPORTUNITY; IF YOU SEE IT, GRASP IT, AND WITH ALL YOUR ENERGY AND WITH ALL YOUR STRENGTH DEVOTE YOURSELF TO THIS TASK."

—Seneca, *Moral Letters to Lucilius*

GO FULL THROTTLE ON WHAT'S GIVEN TO YOU.

Don't squander opportunities when they lay themselves out for the taking. Seize them and put in the sweat to transform them to their full potential. Success is opportunity and dedication combined—use this formula to your advantage.

STOIC EXERCISE ●

Gratitude: Keep it simple. Jot down five things you are grateful for today.

THE STOIC TRANSLATOR

Defeatist Mind: "Death is scary and unknown, so I will avoid risk, connection, and opportunity."

Stoic Mind: "Death is an eventuality, but life is in front of me. I can see, touch, hear, and take part in what life has to offer right now."

"VERY LITTLE INDEED IS NECESSARY FOR LIVING A HAPPY LIFE."

—Marcus Aurelius, *Meditations*

HAPPINESS IS SPARTAN.

Value simplicity like it is the rarest treasure in the world.

The dopamine rush of shiny reward is a short-term high. Enjoy small moments, look for value in the pillars around you, and zero in on what you can't live without.

STOIC EXERCISE ●

Experience nature today. Find a green space—whether it's a park, a forest, or a garden—and go for a walk. Avoid distractions and focus only on the experience of the sights and sounds around you.

"WHEN THIS FACULTY OF THE WILL IS SET RIGHT, A MAN WHO IS NOT GOOD BECOMES GOOD; WHEN IT FAILS, A MAN BECOMES BAD."

—Epictetus, *Discourses*

INTENTION IS NINE-TENTHS OF THE LAW.

No matter which path you're on, you can always turn the car around.
Make the decision every day to set yourself on a good path, and don't
let distractions veer you off course.

STOIC EXERCISE ⬤

Take an inventory of your ethical dilemmas. When in the past have
you made decisions that didn't sit right with you or someone else? How
can you use this experience to correct course in the future?

"MEN ARE
DISTURBED
NOT BY THINGS,
BUT BY THE
VIEWS WHICH
THEY TAKE
OF THINGS."

—Epictetus, *The Enchiridion*

| TODAY'S STOIC READING
The Enchiridion, 5
—EPICTETUS

YOU HAVE POWER OVER YOUR REACTIONS.

How you react to struggle, discomfort, inconvenience, or insult is a snapshot of the life you lead. Step back from what's disturbing you and look at it from arm's length. Consider the ripple effect of your reactions and whether these reactions are rational or flooded with emotion, proportional or outsized.

STOIC EXERCISE

Look at everything with a bird's eye. Consider your most recent stressor or frustration and look at it from above. How does this affect you and those involved? Fly higher. How does it affect your community or the people you love? Increase that altitude. What does it mean for the rest of your life? Use this point-of-view process whenever you make decisions.

"GO ABOUT EVERY ACTION AS YOUR LAST ACTION."

—Marcus Aurelius, *Meditations*

MAKE IT COUNT.

Endeavor to have all of your actions live up to the person you want to be. Make choices you'd be proud of if you didn't have a redo. It's not about hitting every moment out of the park, but showing up to the plate.

STOIC EXERCISE

Journal Reflection: Consider the hurdles you face when endeavoring to be the truest version of yourself. What are they and how much discipline would you need to clear them? Identify what's hard. Decide on one thing to do differently that could make these hurdles seem more surmountable.

THIS STOIC IN HISTORY

Viktor Frankl A Holocaust survivor and psychiatrist, Viktor Frankl developed logotherapy, a form of existential analysis rooted in the belief that finding meaning in life is crucial for enduring suffering. His lesson: Even in the most severe circumstances, you can find purpose and maintain inner freedom through your response to adversity.

"DO NOT ADMIRE YOUR CLOTHES, AND THEN YOU WILL NOT BE ANGRY WITH THE THIEF."

—Epictetus, *Discourses*

| TODAY'S STOIC READING
|
| *Discourses,* 1.18
| —EPICTETUS

FREE YOURSELF FROM THE SHACKLES OF MATERIALISM.

Attachment to meaningless objects sets you up for disappointment.

Count the blessings of your necessities, but reject the notion that belongings contribute to your intrinsic value.

STOIC EXERCISE ●

Today is a minimalist day. Use few possessions throughout your day and focus on necessities only. Avoid luxuries, treats, or cheats, and reflect on how you feel about being successful in restraint.

"THE MOST DISGRACEFUL KIND OF LOSS IS THAT DUE TO CARELESSNESS."

—Seneca, *Moral Letters to Lucilius*

FAILURE HURTS THE MOST WHEN YOU DROP THE BALL.

With scrupulousness comes satisfaction. Don't let ego make you lazy or entitled. Put in the effort and you'll avoid disappointment.

STOIC EXERCISE ●

Do Hard Things: Make the figurative literal with a ball-drop challenge. Using a medicine ball, basketball, or other object that you can hold out in front of you, test your fortitude. Hold the ball or object out straight with both hands, elbows slightly bent, for as long as you can. Use a timer to see how far you can make it before you drop the ball.

"AS A CHANNEL FROM THE
SPRING, YOU YOURSELF
FLOWED: AND THAT THERE
IS BUT A CERTAIN LIMIT OF
TIME APPOINTED TO YOU,
WHICH IF YOU SHOULD NOT
MAKE USE OF TO CALM
AND ALLAY THE MANY
DISTEMPERS OF YOUR SOUL,
IT WILL PASS AWAY AND
YOU WITH IT, AND NEVER
AFTER RETURN."

—Marcus Aurelius, *Meditations*

TODAY'S STOIC READING

Meditations, 2.1
—MARCUS AURELIUS

MAKE GOOD ON YOUR RELATIONSHIP WITH TIME.

Time is flowing but finite. Use the hours given to you to reconcile turmoil and invigorate your soul. Let time be the water that you absorb to nourish you, not the sand that falls through your fingers.

STOIC EXERCISE ●

Scholarly Pause: Test your ability to remain open to differing opinions. Choose to read more deeply into the writings of someone with whom you do not agree for thirty minutes today. Resist the urge to rebuff the content or jump to conclusions.

"BUT THE TYRANT
WILL CHAIN—WHAT?
THE LEG. HE WILL
TAKE AWAY—WHAT?
THE NECK. WHAT
THEN WILL HE NOT
CHAIN AND NOT
TAKE AWAY?
THE WILL."

—Epictetus, *Discourses*

SPIRIT IS AN INFINITE RESOURCE.

Your detractors can make life harder, but they can't take away your drive. Let your inner motivation sustain you when the going gets tough, and you'll find yourself soon on the other side.

STOIC EXERCISE ●

Cold Plunge: 2 minutes. Practice endurance in the face of adversity through cold water therapy. Fill a bathtub with cold water and ice. Sit in the chill for two minutes and strengthen your mind against the things that test you.

"CERTAIN MOMENTS ARE TORN FROM US, SOME ARE GENTLY REMOVED, AND OTHERS GLIDE BEYOND OUR REACH."

—Seneca, *Moral Letters to Lucilius*

TODAY'S STOIC READING

Moral Letters to Lucilius, 1.1
—SENECA

ENDURE MISSED OPPORTUNITY.

It may be stolen from you, it may find a better home, or it may never land in front of you. But how you react to this is far more important than ruminating on what could have been. Missed moments lead to lived moments.

STOIC EXERCISE ●

Live in the moment. Do a social media fast, removing apps from your devices so you are not tempted to break the fast (phones, computers, television, etc.). Exercise self-control and mindfulness by detaching from digital distractions and focusing on the present.

"TO ACT
AGAINST ONE
ANOTHER...
IS CONTRARY
TO NATURE."

—Marcus Aurelius, *Meditations*

TEAMWORK MAKES THE DREAM WORK.

A little competition is healthy, but antagonism is poison.

To embrace the natural order is to embrace community. Find ways to create shared experience and build something with others.

STOIC EXERCISE ●

Gratitude: What do you want to be grateful for but perhaps aren't yet? The first step in opening your mind comes with awareness of your limitations.

"IN THOSE MATTERS WHERE YOU HAVE NOT BEEN PREPARED, YOU MAY KEEP QUIET."

—Epictetus, *Discourses*

DAY	TODAY'S STOIC READING
44	*Discourses,* 2.6 —Epictetus

SILENCE IS A VIRTUE.

The wise know when to sit back and listen. When you have nothing to contribute or you haven't done the work, let someone worthy fill in the gaps. You can learn more when you give others the stage.

STOIC EXERCISE ●

Discipline Check: Take a vow of silence today and commit to it. Whether it's for an hour or for the full day, choose an amount of time that is uncomfortable. Sit in this discomfort and observe.

"I SHOULD PREFER TO LACK SUCCESS RATHER THAN TO LACK FAITH."

—Seneca, *Moral Letters to Lucilius*

TODAY'S STOIC READING

Moral Letters to Lucilius, 25.2
—SENECA

RAISE THE PULSE OF YOUR BEATING HOPE.

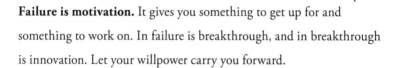

Failure is motivation. It gives you something to get up for and something to work on. In failure is breakthrough, and in breakthrough is innovation. Let your willpower carry you forward.

STOIC EXERCISE ●

Don a thick skin and look for critical feedback today. Be receptive to the idea that understanding your failures is a building block to something greater. There is no such thing as excellence without trial and error.

A MODERN SPOTLIGHT

Samuel Beckett The Irish playwright emulated persistence and creativity with the axiom, "Try again, fail again, fail better," from *Worstward Ho*. This philosophy strives to accept failure as an opportunity for growth, persist through challenges, and continuously endeavor to improve with each effort.

"LET THE WRONG WHICH IS DONE BY A MAN STAY THERE WHERE THE WRONG WAS DONE."

—Marcus Aurelius, *Meditations*

TODAY'S STOIC READING

Meditations, 7.29
—Marcus Aurelius

LET IT LIE.

Don't get bogged down by past transgressions.

Move forward and onward. When you can't find it in yourself
to forgive, you carry the weight with you wherever you go.
Give your spine a break.

STOIC EXERCISE ●

Letting go lets you off the hook. How has forgiveness—even if
you weren't quite ready for it—released a burden? What are five
things you would like to feel or experience if you didn't have the
burden of resentment?

"CONSIDER HOW MUCH MORE FRUGAL ARE THE POOR THAN WE, AND HOW MUCH MORE PATIENT OF HARDSHIP."

—Epictetus, *The Echiridion*

TODAY'S STOIC READING

The Echiridion, 67
—EPICTETUS

NEVER LOSE PERSPECTIVE.

Suffering is relative, but consider the hardship of others.

When you indulge petty grievances, you indulge your ego. Make it a practice to remind yourself of your true needs versus your wants.

STOIC EXERCISE

Journal Reflection: In your written reflection today, think of a current frustration that has been hovering over you. When you zoom out, is it still as problematic as it feels in the moment? What reminders can you carry with you when you need a perspective shift? Reflect on what makes you fortunate in spite of this issue.

"I SHALL ENJOY LIFE JUST BECAUSE I AM NOT OVER-ANXIOUS AS TO THE FUTURE DATE OF MY DEPARTURE."

—Seneca, *Moral Letters to Lucilius*

| DAY **48** | TODAY'S STOIC READING
Moral Letters to Lucilius, 61.2
—SENECA |

TO WORRY IS TO SUFFER TWICE.

The end of things is inevitable, including death. But to dwell in fear of the end is to dismiss the joys right in front of you. Embrace the life shining on you at this moment and set the fears aside.

STOIC EXERCISE ●

Do Hard Things: Ask uncomfortable questions. Use the opportunity to make plans in the event of catastrophe, illness, or unexpected life changes. Treat sensitive subjects like battles to be strategized.

"WITHIN IS THE FOUNTAIN OF GOOD, AND IT WILL EVER BUBBLE UP, IF YOU WILL EVER DIG."

—Marcus Aurelius, *Meditations*

TODAY'S STOIC READING

Meditations, 7.59
—MARCUS AURELIUS

FULFILLMENT IS THERE IF YOU STRIVE FOR IT.

Good fortune and inner satisfaction are ever-flowing, should you choose to put in the work. Go beyond the surface of things and be willing to hustle for what matters. There is no reward in laziness.

STOIC EXERCISE ●

Breathwork: Do a session of breathwork before you start your day. Use an app or video to guide you based on whether you want to reduce stress, feel energized, or clear your mind.

"IF YOU EVER WISH TO EXERCISE YOURSELF IN LABOR AND ENDURANCE, DO IT FOR YOURSELF, NOT OTHERS."

—Epictetus, *The Echiridion*

EFFORT IS FOR YOU, NOT FOR SHOW.

Working hard to draw attention to yourself is more energy than working hard for yourself. When you rise to a challenge, be ready to honor your effort silently and without expectation of others.

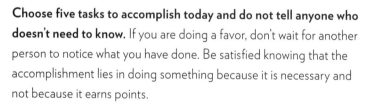

STOIC EXERCISE

Choose five tasks to accomplish today and do not tell anyone who doesn't need to know. If you are doing a favor, don't wait for another person to notice what you have done. Be satisfied knowing that the accomplishment lies in doing something because it is necessary and not because it earns points.

"THAT WHICH IS BOUND TO BE A NECESSITY IF YOU REBEL, IS NOT A NECESSITY IF YOU DESIRE IT."

—Seneca, *Moral Letters to Lucilius*

TODAY'S STOIC READING

Moral Letters to Lucilius, 61.3
—Seneca

ALIGN YOUR DESIRES WITH THE INEVITABLE.

Suffering happens when you rebel against necessity. Resist the temptation to reject inevitability and instead embrace it. When you look forward to what already is, it will never feel like a burden.

STOIC EXERCISE

Scholarly Pause: Choose a pillar of Stoicism with which you struggle the most. Find an article, text, or podcast to focus on for thirty minutes that will allow you to more directly connect with this concept.

AN EYE ON THE PHILOSOPHER

Seneca the Younger (c. 4 BCE–65 CE), or Lucius Annaeus Seneca, was a Roman philosopher, statesman, and playwright whose perspective made Stoicism accessible to modern thinkers. His philosophy: exude self-control, live by a strong moral compass, be in harmony with the natural order of things, and face adversity with resilience.

"IF YOU ARE PAINED BY ANY EXTERNAL THING, IT IS NOT THIS THING THAT DISTURBS YOU, BUT YOUR OWN JUDGMENT ABOUT IT."

—Marcus Aurelius, *Meditations*

YOU ARE NOT WHAT HAPPENS TO YOU.

Pain will come and injustices will find you. But these moments do not need to determine the full course of your life. How you choose to react to the things that upset you paves the road ahead.

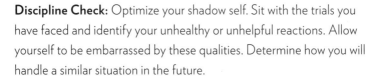

STOIC EXERCISE

Discipline Check: Optimize your shadow self. Sit with the trials you have faced and identify your unhealthy or unhelpful reactions. Allow yourself to be embarrassed by these qualities. Determine how you will handle a similar situation in the future.

"WHEN YOU HAVE SUCH HANDS, DO YOU STILL LOOK FOR ONE WHO SHALL WIPE YOUR NOSE?"

—Epictetus, *Discourses*

GROW UP AND SHOW UP.

You have it in you to succeed. When you have the tools in front of you, use them. Don't expect others to baby you if you are capable of the same effort. Find satisfaction in making things happen.

STOIC EXERCISE ●

Gratitude: What tools or gifts are you grateful to have? Consider five and how they have helped you along the way.

THIS STOIC IN HISTORY

Queen Elizabeth II As the longest-reigning British monarch, Queen Elizabeth II demonstrated Stoic principles through her unwavering sense of duty, composure, and resilience in the face of personal and national challenges. Throughout her reign, she remained a steadfast symbol of stability and continuity, handling crises with grace and a calm demeanor. A lesson from the queen: Maintain your responsibilities with dedication, remain composed under pressure, and lead with a steady hand and a clear mind.

"DEMAND NOT THAT EVENTS SHOULD HAPPEN AS YOU WISH; BUT WISH THEM TO HAPPEN AS THEY DO."

—Epictetus, *The Enchiridion*

HAPPINESS ISN'T ABOUT GETTING WHAT YOU WANT.

It's about finding the benefit in what you have been given.

Connecting your desires to your contentment is the materialism of the soul. It will leave you feeling unsatisfied if you don't attain it and leave you wanting more if you do. Take care of what's already in hand.

STOIC EXERCISE ●

Think of every innovation in the history of the universe. Each was a solution to a problem. What's one you admire or can't live without? Keep it in your back pocket for when something doesn't go your way. Pull it out and remind yourself that there's an opportunity ahead.

"WHEN YOU ARE OFFENDED WITH ANY MAN'S TRANSGRESSION, PRESENTLY REFLECT UPON YOURSELF AND CONSIDER WHAT YOU YOURSELF ARE GUILTY OF IN THE SAME KIND."

—Marcus Aurelius, *Meditations*

IF YOU BUILD A GLASS HOUSE, MAKE SURE IT'S MADE OF MIRRORS.

Watch your judgment. Reflect on your own actions before you throw stones. Use the stones to build a stronger house that you can be proud of. Show compassion to those who make mistakes, and invite them in.

STOIC EXERCISE ●

Meditation: 20 minutes. Find a quiet space. Sit upright in silence or with white noise. Relax your body and let your palms rest on your knees. If you feel tension, sit in the discomfort. Let it wash over you until it evens out and your mind clears.

"WHOEVER THEN UNDERSTANDS WHAT IS GOOD, CAN ALSO KNOW HOW TO LOVE."

—Epictetus, *Discourses*

LOVE IS WHEN GOOD MEETS LOGIC.

Love is the center of everything, and it's burdened only by ego and selfishness. When you follow the steps to put good into the world, love fills in the empty spaces.

STOIC EXERCISE

Unlock your capacity to love for neighbors and strangers. Find a local charity, organization, or mentorship program that you believe in and take a direct action to contribute your time in person.

"THERE IS GREAT PLEASURE, NOT ONLY IN MAINTAINING OLD AND ESTABLISHED FRIENDSHIPS, BUT ALSO IN BEGINNING AND ACQUIRING NEW ONES."

—Seneca, *Moral Letters to Lucilius*

FRIENDSHIP IS AN ETERNAL POWER SOURCE.

You derive energy from your healthiest friendships. Tend to the ones that continue to grow and seek out new ones. When the spark of new friendship is made, you find reinvigorated momentum.

STOIC EXERCISE ●

Journal Reflection: Consider your friendships. Which ones still feel aligned and healthy? Which ones feel like they have veered off course? If you are eager for new friendships, determine one activity you could do or resource you could optimize to find them.

"ADORN YOURSELF WITH SIMPLICITY AND MODESTY."

—Marcus Aurelius, *Meditations*

DAY	TODAY'S STOIC READING
58	*Meditations,* 7.31 —Marcus Aurelius

NOT ALL TREASURE IS GOLD.

Humility is the reward. Focus on what is essential, what is important, and what doesn't draw unnecessary attention. To avoid vanity will cost your ego but will build the wealth of your integrity.

STOIC EXERCISE ●

Do Hard Things: Create an embargo on nonessential purchases. Choose a time frame, whether it's one week, one month, or a full year. Spend money only on the things you absolutely need and learn to reject everything else. You will feel lighter.

"WHEN YOU DO ANYTHING FROM A CLEAR JUDGMENT THAT IT OUGHT TO BE DONE, NEVER SHRINK FROM BEING SEEN TO DO IT, EVEN THOUGH THE WORLD SHOULD MISUNDERSTAND IT."

—Epictetus, *The Echiridion*

DO THE RIGHT THING, EVEN IF IT'S UNPOPULAR.

Keep that backbone firm. Others may not understand your motivations, but history will always offer the final judgment. Muster the strength to do what's right, even if you're going against the tide.

STOIC EXERCISE ●

Don't fall back into the shadows because it's easier. Stand up for someone who needs it today or when you see it soon. A respectful but firm word of support can make the difference for someone who needs it.

THE STOIC TRANSLATOR

Victim Mind: "Why do bad things always happen to me? It's so unfair."
Stoic Mind: "Adversity is a part of life. I'll use this challenge as an opportunity to grow stronger and wiser."

"WHAT BENEFIT
IS THERE IN
REVIEWING PAST
SUFFERINGS, AND
IN BEING UNHAPPY,
JUST BECAUSE
ONCE YOU WERE
UNHAPPY?"

—Seneca, *Moral Letters to Lucilius*

DWELL ON UNHAPPINESS AND YOU'LL ENSURE UNHAPPINESS.

To drown yourself in the memory of despair only hinders you from feeling the fresh air of future happiness. Accept the disappointments of the past and use this motivation to try again.

STOIC EXERCISE ●

Scholarly Pause: Sometimes you don't know what you need. Choose a topic you know nothing about and read about it for thirty minutes. Let yourself go down the rabbit hole in pursuit of knowledge.

"LOOK ROUND AT THE COURSES OF THE STARS, AS IF YOU WERE GOING ALONG WITH THEM."

—Marcus Aurelius, *Meditations*

	TODAY'S STOIC READING
	Meditations, 7.47
	—MARCUS AURELIUS

FIND AWE IN THE RHYTHM OF THE UNIVERSE.

Transcend petty concerns and recognize the greater order of nature.

Let the vastness and interconnectedness of the cosmos be a reminder to realign your perspective when you have trouble seeing the way.

STOIC EXERCISE ●

Cold Plunge: 4 minutes. Find peace in a test of wills with cold water therapy. Fill a bathtub with cold water and ice. Sit in the chill for four minutes, breathing fully and deeply, and embrace the serenity of your body's natural ability to adapt.

"NOTHING GREAT IS CREATED SUDDENLY."

—Epictetus, *Discourses*

BE PATIENT IN YOUR PURSUITS.

Michelangelo's statue *David* wasn't carved with a stick of dynamite. Greatness comes with fastidious attention and dogged patience. Craft your goals by chipping away and polishing over time, not by showing up with a bang.

STOIC EXERCISE ●

Discipline Check: Choose a goal and make a calendar, checklist, or time-blocking system that will allow you to do a little bit every day. Make this process so easy it's nearly invisible, and then chip away.

"YOUR GREATEST DIFFICULTY IS WITH YOURSELF; FOR YOU ARE YOUR OWN STUMBLING BLOCK."

—Seneca, *Moral Letters to Lucilius*

INSECURITY IS A STEPPING-STONE TO PASS, NOT A WALL TO CLIMB.

Learn from the fear inside you, but recognize that fear is a construct of the mind. Invigorate your mind with the will to move beyond the fear, to take the first step. Then another. And another.

STOIC EXERCISE ●

Gratitude: Keep it simple. Jot down five things you are grateful for today.

"HOW
MIRACULOUSLY
THINGS CONTRARY
TO ONE ANOTHER,
CONCUR TO THE
BEAUTY AND
PERFECTION
OF THIS UNIVERSE."

—Marcus Aurelius, *Meditations*

DAY	TODAY'S STOIC READING
64	*Meditations,* 7.26 —Marcus Aurelius

FIND BEAUTY IN DIFFERENCES.

Puzzle pieces only form a picture if opposites come together.
Understand that there is no light without darkness, there is no balance
without weight and counterweight, and there is no growth without an
open mind toward the unfamiliar.

STOIC EXERCISE ●

**Engage in a respectful philosophical conversation with someone
today.** Show curiosity for their opinion and treat the exchange as
an opportunity to discover new ideas and opinions rather than
a debate to win.

"IF YOU WOULD IMPROVE, BE CONTENT TO BE THOUGHT FOOLISH AND DULL."

—Epictetus, *The Echiridion*

TODAY'S STOIC READING

The Echiridion, 13
—Epictetus

RESPECT THE GRIND, EVEN IF OTHERS DON'T RESPECT YOU.

Improvement doesn't happen in a vacuum. Be prepared to be the butt of the joke while you hustle. The reward is in the forward momentum, and it may take others a while to catch up.

STOIC EXERCISE ●

Commit to a new skill that lands outside of your comfort zone.
Whether it's a hobby or an area of expertise that feels out of your reach, decide that it's okay for you to mess up while doing it and try anyway.

"HE WHO BEGINS TO BE YOUR FRIEND BECAUSE IT PAYS WILL ALSO CEASE BECAUSE IT PAYS."

—Seneca, *Moral Letters to Lucilius*

| TODAY'S STOIC READING

Moral Letters to Lucilius, 9.9
—Seneca

A TRUE FRIEND IS THERE IN PAIN OR GAIN.

Friends in low places bring you down to low places. Focus on friendships that offer intrinsic value rather than convenience and you'll never be lonely.

STOIC EXERCISE ●

How do you or others in your circles treat those who cannot offer you anything? Recognize that integrity is strongest in the person who treats everyone respectfully, not transactionally.

THIS STOIC IN HISTORY

Eleanor Roosevelt American political figure, activist, and 32nd First Lady of the United States , Eleanor Roosevelt didn't suffer fools. She said, "A snub is the effort of a person who feels superior to make someone else feel inferior. To do so, he has to find someone who can be made to feel inferior."

"WE ARE MADE FOR COOPERATION, LIKE FEET, LIKE HANDS, LIKE EYELIDS."

—Marcus Aurelius, *Meditations*

DAY	TODAY'S STOIC READING
67	*Meditations*, 2.1 —Marcus Aurelius

IN COLLABORATION THERE IS LIFE ITSELF.

Individuality is a strength; individualism is a failure of potential.

Embrace the natural alignment of duality. Let help come your way and offer help in return. Discover the satisfaction of work done together.

STOIC EXERCISE

Journal Reflection: Think outwardly in your gratitude. Who is someone who has helped you unexpectedly or joined in to collaborate with you to yield a success? What makes giving or receiving help a necessary pursuit?

"BE NOT VEXED IF OTHERS HAVE THE ADVANTAGE OVER YOU."

—Epictetus, *Discourses*

A SENSE OF INADEQUACY IS A YOU PROBLEM.

No one is strong in all things. When someone else has the advantage, congratulate them and find a different lane. To be self-pitying about another's strength is to miss the opportunity to make up for their weaknesses.

STOIC EXERCISE ●

Do Hard Things: Compliment your adversary. Dig as deep as you can to find redeeming qualities in someone you dislike. No one is all bad or all good. Find a strand of positivity that someone else may see in that person and grab onto it.

"YOU MUST BE NOT ONLY PRESENT IN THE BODY, BUT WATCHFUL IN MIND, IF YOU WOULD AVAIL YOURSELF OF THE FLEETING OPPORTUNITY."

—Seneca, *Moral Letters to Lucilius*

DAY 69

KEEP YOUR HEAD IN THE GAME.

Brute force alone won't move you forward, but the clarity of mind to keep going will. Be alert in all things and recognize when a flickering prospect gleams in front of you. Have the sharpness of mind to know to take it.

STOIC EXERCISE ●

Be fully present in an experience today. Enjoy a meal with zero distractions and track your thoughts, tastes, and sensations, or listen to a long piece of music with full attention and be alert in how the sounds or lyrics affect you.

"TAKE PLEASURE IN ONE THING AND REST IN IT."

—Marcus Aurelius, *Meditations*

REVEL IN SINGULARITY.

You can collect as many distractions as you like, but to truly appreciate something, you have to marinate in it. Focus on one joy and study it. Unravel its meaning. Look at it from all angles. Find meaning in simplicity and in commitment.

STOIC EXERCISE ●

Scholarly Pause: Ruminate on a Stoic concept you wish to emulate. Read about it for thirty minutes today without the presence of distractions.

"IT IS THE ACTION OF AN UNINSTRUCTED PERSON TO REPROACH OTHERS FOR HIS OWN MISFORTUNES."

—Epictetus, *The Echiridion*

BLAME IS A GAME FOR THE UNWISE.

Practice self-reflection before you lash out. Decide whether finger-pointing is the correct pursuit and question the genesis of the blame altogether. If it can be directed back to you, you won't enjoy the irony.

STOIC EXERCISE

Tap into a perspective shift. Spend the day seeing things from someone else's point of view. Choose someone with whom you don't often agree or whose processing is different from yours.

"GOOD LUCK FREES MANY MEN FROM PUNISHMENT, BUT NO MAN FROM FEAR."

—Seneca, *Moral Letters to Lucilius*

TODAY'S STOIC READING

Moral Letters to Lucilius, 97.16
—SENECA

GOOD FORTUNE IS A TEMPORARY SALVE.

There is a rush of relief in skating by, in evading consequences, or in not being found out. But external factors can never fully alleviate fear. The fear that comeuppance will find you remains, and your conscience is always at work. Inner fortitude is the lasting fortune.

STOIC EXERCISE ●

Discipline Check: Face your fears. What are you not owning up to, communicating, or addressing? Identify something you have been avoiding and put a plan into action to address it.

THE STOIC TRANSLATOR

Selfish Mind: "That's not my problem. I'm just going to focus on what's good for me."
Stoic Mind: "It's not all about me. The bigger picture matters."

"LOOK IN, LET NOT EITHER THE PROPER QUALITY, OR THE TRUE WORTH OF ANYTHING PASS YOU."

—Marcus Aurelius, *Meditations*

TODAY'S STOIC READING

Meditations, 6.3
—MARCUS AURELIUS

IDENTIFY SINCERITY AND HOLD ONTO IT.

Look closely, be thoughtful, and assess people and things for their earnest qualities. Don't be distracted by the gleam of surface-level shine. True gold runs deep.

STOIC EXERCISE ●

Gratitude: What or whom do you appreciate for their transparency? Consider five people or things in your life that you can take at face value and the ways in which this lightens your load.

AN EYE ON THE PHILOSOPHER

Chrysippus (c. 279–206 BCE) succeeded Cleanthes as the head of the Stoic school and significantly advanced Stoic philosophy. He wrote extensively, shaping Stoic logic, ethics, and physics, and is often considered the co-founder of Stoicism. His teachings: Rational understanding and virtuous living are essential for achieving a life in accordance with nature.

"ALWAYS REMEMBER WHAT IS YOUR OWN, AND WHAT BELONGS TO ANOTHER; AND YOU WILL NOT BE DISTURBED."

—Epictetus, *Discourses*

| TODAY'S STOIC READING
| *Discourses,* 2.6
| —Epictetus

REJECT ENVY.

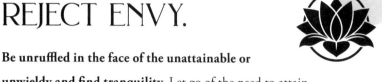

Be unruffled in the face of the unattainable or unwieldy and find tranquility. Let go of the need to attain what has not been presented to you. Find peace in the idea that what is yours is yours and that is all you need.

STOIC EXERCISE

Breathwork: Do a session of breathwork when you feel tension rising up. Set a timer for five minutes and breathe evenly and deeply with your eyes closed.

"REFLECT THAT NOTHING EXCEPT THE SOUL IS WORTHY OF WONDER; FOR TO THE SOUL, IF IT BE GREAT, NAUGHT IS GREAT."

—Seneca, *Moral Letters to Lucilius*

SEEK VIRTUE IN A NOBLE INNER LIFE.

True greatness is internal and enduring, not external and transient.

No matter how impressive external forces may seem, there is nothing that compares to impressive character. Exert energy on building integrity, not wealth.

STOIC EXERCISE ●

Meditation: 30 minutes. Find a quiet space without distractions. Use a meditation app or a white noise machine to guide you through this longer space. Embrace the unknown.

"IT IS IMPOSSIBLE
FOR A MAN TO
BEGIN TO LEARN
THAT WHICH
HE THINKS HE
ALREADY KNOWS."

—Epictetus, *Discourses*

DAY **76**	TODAY'S STOIC READING *Discourses*, 2.17 —EPICTETUS

LEAVE ROOM FOR GROWTH, NOT ARROGANCE.

Possibilities are endless if you believe you always have something to learn. Growth comes from recognizing that education is a lifelong pursuit and that even expertise can be evolved. Remain humble and dismiss the idea that there is no other peak to climb after you reach the top of a mountain.

STOIC EXERCISE ●

Create a learning plan for a topic you're unfamiliar with or recognize you could brush up on. Alternatively, question the assumption that you already know enough about a subject you enjoy and dedicate time to discovering something new.

"EVERYONE ADDS MUCH TO HIS OWN ILLS, AND TELLS LIES TO HIMSELF."

—Seneca, *Moral Letters to Lucilius*

| TODAY'S STOIC READING

Moral Letters to Lucilius, 78.14
—SENECA

RADICAL HONESTY IS BEST USED IN THE MIRROR.

Lie to yourself to feel good right now. Be honest to feel good about yourself tomorrow. The road has enough obstacles without tossing nails in your own path. Be honest with yourself in all that you can and cannot control. Hard choices are often the ones you make for yourself.

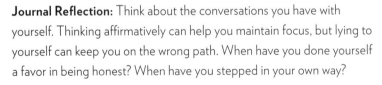

STOIC EXERCISE ●

Journal Reflection: Think about the conversations you have with yourself. Thinking affirmatively can help you maintain focus, but lying to yourself can keep you on the wrong path. When have you done yourself a favor in being honest? When have you stepped in your own way?

"SUMMER
AND WINTER,
AND ABUNDANCE
AND SCARCITY,
AND VIRTUE
AND VICE … ALL
SUCH OPPOSITES
FOR THE HARMONY
OF THE WHOLE."

—Epictetus, *Discourses*

TODAY'S STOIC READING

Discourses, 1.12
—EPICTETUS

TRUST IN THE EQUILIBRIUM OF ALL THINGS.

Welcome what is balanced. Hoarding anything—happiness, passion, objects, desires—will leave you off-kilter. Trust in the natural order of contrast, and that the two sides of a coin are necessary.

STOIC EXERCISE ●

Do Hard Things: Engage in some balance work. Take a yoga class or find an online workout that focuses strictly on balance for at least one full hour. Witness the necessity of equilibrium in your physical space. You cannot do one side of anything without feeling the urge to complete the other.

"THE UNIVERSE IS TRANSFORMATION: LIFE IS OPINION."

—Marcus Aurelius, *Meditations*

DAY	TODAY'S STOIC READING
79	*Meditations, 4.3* —MARCUS AURELIUS

GO WITH THE FLOW.

The universe is impermanent and ever in flux. Change is fundamental and infinite. When the only constant is that very little is within your control, you can find peace in the release. Let go of expectation and let tranquility find you.

STOIC EXERCISE ●

Release your grip today. When you are confronted with a choice, flip a coin or let someone else take the reins. Follow through and assess how it feels not to be in control of everything.

"UNLESS YOU PERFECTLY UNDERSTAND HIS MOTIVES, HOW SHOULD YOU KNOW IF HE ACTS ILL?"

—Epictetus, *The Echiridion*

TODAY'S STOIC READING

The Echiridion, 65
—EPICTETUS

LET ACTIONS SPEAK LOUDER THAN YOUR ASSUMPTIONS.

You never know what's going on in someone else's world.

Resist the urge to jump to conclusions about a person's intentions, especially if these conclusions are convenient. Be patient and let others show you who they are.

STOIC EXERCISE •

Scholarly Pause: Check your assumptions. Spend thirty minutes reading about a topic or a person you may not be giving enough deference to.

"ONE WHO SEEKS
FRIENDSHIP
FOR FAVORABLE
OCCASIONS,
STRIPS IT OF
ALL ITS NOBILITY."

—Seneca, *Moral Letters to Lucilius*

BE AN ALL-WEATHER FRIEND.

Through thick and thin, be the kind of friend others can count on.
The value of a good friendship can be found in its endurance and earnestness. Strike gold by digging deep with your friendships rather than by scraping the surface.

STOIC EXERCISE ●

Check in on your friends today. Ask them earnest questions and resist the urge to chime in with information about yourself. See what happens when you get past the surface.

"TRANQUILITY IS NOTHING ELSE THAN THE GOOD ORDERING OF THE MIND."

—Marcus Aurelius, *Meditations*

FIND PEACE IN DISCIPLINE.

Serenity is yours when you prioritize rational thought, maintain focus, and control your emotions. Let your laser focus on well-sorted thinking to snuff out distractions and unnecessary emotional labor.

STOIC EXERCISE ●

Cold Plunge: 5 minutes. Sit in the chill for five minutes and focus on your ability to clear the cobwebs, embrace discomfort, and arrive at a space of tranquility through hard work.

A MODERN SPOTLIGHT

Warren Buffett Not all Stoics have faces carved in stone. Stoic principles are everywhere. American businessman Warren Buffet didn't become a billionaire by acting recklessly. He is known for patient investing, rational decision-making, and modest living. Buffet still lives in the Omaha, Nebraska, home he purchased in 1958.

"WHO THEN IS
THE INVINCIBLE?
IT IS HE WHOM
NONE OF THE
THINGS DISTURB
WHICH ARE
INDEPENDENT
OF THE WILL."

—Epictetus, *Discourses*

LET GO AND BECOME UNSHAKABLE.

Attempt to control the outcome and the outcome will control you.

Dispel the myth that you can change the course of a car you're not driving. Find resilience in the armor of inevitability.

STOIC EXERCISE ●

Gratitude: What appreciation can you find in letting go? List five times you have identified something as an immovable force, accepted this, and moved on.

"WHAT THEN
IS PECULIAR
TO MAN? REASON.
WHEN THIS IS
RIGHT AND HAS
REACHED
PERFECTION,
MAN'S FELICITY
IS COMPLETE."

—Seneca, *Moral Letters to Lucilius*

TODAY'S STOIC READING

Moral Letters to Lucilius, 76.10
—SENECA

HAPPINESS IS THE EVOLUTION OF REASON.

Your ability to parse, ruminate, and logic your way through anything makes you human. Strive to build this muscle through practice, and you will get closer to satisfaction with every repetition.

STOIC EXERCISE ●

Discipline Check: Work through hard puzzles. Complete a crossword, puzzle, or brain game as a way to stretch your logic muscles.

"GIVE YOURSELF TIME TO LEARN SOMETHING NEW AND GOOD, AND CEASE TO BE WHIRLED AROUND."

—Marcus Aurelius, *Meditations*

| | TODAY'S STOIC READING |

Meditations, 2.7
—Marcus Aurelius

FIND PURPOSE IN SELF-IMPROVEMENT.

Learning is a lifelong endeavor. Invigorate the mind, collect knowledge, and test your ability to reason with a steady flow of knowledge. Chaotic distractions and dizzying stressors fade away when you keep your eye on the prize.

STOIC EXERCISE ●

Let your pursuit of knowledge travel. Be curious about another culture and make a plan to visit the location or to study it in depth. Learn about cultural practices different from your own and investigate the art, music, and storytelling of the place.

"DO NOT EMBRACE STATUES."

—Epictetus, *The Echiridion*

SUPERFICIALITY IS A FALSE GOD.

Status and appearances get you only so far. Reject the emphasis society places on materialism and meaningless symbols of worth. Focus on inner values rather than external optics.

STOIC EXERCISE ●

Be forensic about your finances so that you can access a more mindful and sustainable lifestyle. Exercise discipline and self-control in managing your money and identify unnecessary expenses. Commit to reducing them.

AN EYE ON THE PHILOSOPHER

Epictetus (c. 50–135 CE), from the Greek, *Epíktētos*, means "acquired." He was born enslaved yet became a leading voice of Stoicism. His philosophy: Identify what is within your control and what isn't and find happiness in acceptance.

"A GOOD DISPOSITION IS INVINCIBLE IF IT BE GENUINE."

—Marcus Aurelius, *Meditations*

POSITIVITY IS A PASSPORT.

A good attitude will take you far. Embrace sincerity and a positive mindset whenever you can, but you do not need to go so far as to be phony. The slightest uplifting outlook can move mountains.

STOIC EXERCISE

Journal Reflection: Continue your writing practice. Consider how positive people in your life or a shift in perspective when you needed it has helped you. When have you opened the door to something better and it walked right in?

"WE SUFFER MORE OFTEN IN IMAGINATION THAN IN REALITY."

—Seneca, *Moral Letters to Lucilius*

TODAY'S STOIC READING

Moral Letters to Lucilius, 13.4
—Seneca

FEAR IS CREATIVITY GONE AWRY.

Your imagination can take you to some wild places, but you don't have to go along for the ride. Don't let the concern of what could be interfere with what is. Value what is within your control and strengthen the muscle that deflects outlandish worries.

STOIC EXERCISE ●

Do Hard Things: Sign up for an activity, race, or event that pushes your boundaries. Whether you dislike public speaking, team sports, or even changes to your routine, find something that challenges you and face it.

"SET YOURSELF FREE
FOR YOUR OWN SAKE;
GATHER AND SAVE
YOUR TIME, WHICH
TILL LATELY HAS BEEN
FORCED FROM YOU,
OR FILCHED AWAY,
OR HAS MERELY
SLIPPED FROM
YOUR HANDS."

—Seneca, *Moral Letters to Lucilius*

DAY 89	TODAY'S STOIC READING
	Moral Letters to Lucilius, 1.1
	—SENECA

RECLAIM YOUR TIME FROM THE FORCES THAT WASTE IT.

Be mindful of how you use your time because it is not an endless well. To waste time is to disrespect your own principles. Pull from your well of discipline instead, and use the time allotted to you as if it were a precious resource.

STOIC EXERCISE ●

Set five achievable goals today. Create a time-blocking schedule in which you silence distractions for a set period of time—be it five minutes or an hour—and clock yourself while you focus on the goal. Blocking out your calendar and committing to these goals will help you knock them off your list.

"PURE LOVE, CARELESS OF ALL OTHER THINGS, KINDLES THE SOUL WITH DESIRE FOR THE BEAUTIFUL OBJECT, NOT WITHOUT THE HOPE OF A RETURN OF THE AFFECTION."

—Seneca, *Moral Letters to Lucilius*

SELFLESS LOVE TRANSCENDS ALL.

Pure love exists for the sake of love itself. The underlying hope for a love returned is perfectly human, but offer that love without expectation. Let love ignite your heart with good intention.

STOIC EXERCISE ●

Practice reducing your expectations of others. Endeavor to perform five selfless acts this week, from something as small as pouring a cup of coffee for a loved one to something bigger, like being there for someone in a time of need. Do these things without looking for gratitude. Find satisfaction in quiet kindness.

A MODERN SPOTLIGHT

Malala Yousafzai The Nobel Peace Prize laureate Malala Yousafzai survived an assassination attempt by the Taliban, yet still champions girls' education with an unwavering spirit. Malala's principles are clear: Stand firm in your convictions and use your voice for change.

"THE SOUL IS DYED BY THE THOUGHTS."

—Marcus Aurelius, *Meditations*

THE QUALITY OF YOUR THOUGHTS DETERMINES THE QUALITY OF YOUR SOUL.

Think negative thoughts, and you will live negativity. Think positive thoughts, and you will live positively. Emotion is understandably fickle, but allowing negativity to loiter within your inner world will corrupt your ability to live peacefully. Let your thoughts be dyed with good.

STOIC EXERCISE

Scholarly Pause: Read a great work of literature for one hour. Choose something you read in the past or one you have always been meaning to read. Remove all distractions so you truly focus in on the experience.

"THE MIND
MAINTAINS
ITS OWN
TRANQUILITY
BY RETIRING
INTO ITSELF."

—Marcus Aurelius, *Meditations*

TODAY'S STOIC READING

Meditations, 7.33
—Marcus Aurelius

YOUR MIND IS A SANCTUARY.

When everyday noise gets too loud, turn inward. The mind is your most powerful paradise, with its own ability to preserve tranquility and savor rest. Tune into your inner world, practice self-reflection, and recognize that true serenity comes from within.

STOIC EXERCISE ●

Discipline Check: Exert effort from the body to train the mind. Push through your fitness routine today without distractions like music, screens, or external affirmations. Be present in your thoughts.

"NEVER PROCLAIM YOURSELF A PHILOSOPHER... BUT SHOW THEM BY ACTIONS."

—Epictetus, *The Echiridion*

WISDOM IS SET TO LOW VOLUME.

Practice your principles and inner philosophy rather than prattling about it to others. To announce yourself is to open yourself up to criticism if you don't follow through. To show who you are is to prove your integrity.

STOIC EXERCISE ●

Gratitude: Show up in your acknowledgment of the things that aid you. Write a list of five things that have pushed you to be a better, more integrity-focused version of yourself.

"THE OUTCOME OF A MIGHTY ANGER IS MADNESS."

—Seneca, *Moral Letters to Lucilius*

TODAY'S STOIC READING

Moral Letters to Lucilius, 18.15
—SENECA

UNCHECKED RAGE YIELDS SELF-DESTRUCTION.

Consider the rational outcome of anger untethered: chaos.

Find catharsis in regulating your emotions rather than following them down a dark path. There is peace in discipline and in control.

STOIC EXERCISE ●

Unlock meditative practices in moments of stress. Clear your mind. Breathe deeply. Imagine yourself in a cool, dark chamber far from the fire you're currently facing. Count to ten and imagine the feeling of freedom in being above and away from the issue.

"FIRST SAY TO YOURSELF WHO YOU WISH TO BE, THEN DO ACCORDINGLY."

—Epictetus, *Discourses*

DAY	TODAY'S STOIC READING
95	*Discourses*, 3.23 —Epictetus

AFFIRM YOUR CHARACTER BY LIVING IT.

Set your intention for who you wish to be and how you wish to live.
Treat it like arithmetic and consider the calculations. Find the values
you need to be your highest self and live them to add up to the whole.

<hr>

STOIC EXERCISE ●

Meditation: 1 hour. Accept challenges that are presented to you. You
can handle it. Embrace the emptiness of a clear mind and relaxed body
for a full hour, and don't let yourself get pulled away by outside stimuli.

"SOLID TIMBERS HAVE REPELLED A VERY GREAT FIRE. DRY AND EASILY FLAMMABLE STUFF NOURISHES THE SLIGHTEST SPARK INTO A CONFLAGRATION."

—Seneca, *Moral Letters to Lucilius*

INNER STRENGTH FORTIFIES YOUR SOUL.

Build your character with solid materials. Follow your principles according to the blueprint that makes you the person you want to be. Don't let minor challenges and lack of preparation destroy what you've worked for.

STOIC EXERCISE

Breathwork: Utilize deep breathing today. When small challenges come up, diffuse the situation with even breathing that clears everything away.

THIS STOIC IN HISTORY

George Washington In a blistering winter between 1777 and 1778, the Revolutionary War was raging at the Valley Forge encampment. More than 2,000 troops died of illness, morale was low, and food and supplies were scarce. But George Washington, an admirer of Stoicism, turned the war around. Washington's lesson: Through self-control, endurance, and discipline, leadership can turn the tide.

"HOW SHALL I NOT BE ANXIOUS?' FOOL, HAVE YOU NOT HANDS?"

—Epictetus, *Discourses*

TODAY'S STOIC READING

Discourses, 2.16
—Epictetus

EMPOWER YOUR MIND WITH YOUR OWN STRENGTHS.

Ease your anxious mind with your personal stockpile of resources.
Acknowledge your strengths and make a plan to break down the
manageable parts using them. Reinvigorate your confidence and
your drive in order to overcome anxious thoughts.

STOIC EXERCISE ●

Journal Reflection: Do a free-write of the worries that plague your
thoughts and the doomsday ramifications if they were to unfold. Strike a
line through this afterward. Next, make a list of your strengths, and write
about how you can fight off your concerns using this arsenal.

"YOU OUGHT TO MAKE YOURSELF OF A DIFFERENT STAMP FROM THE MULTITUDE."

—Seneca, *Moral Letters to Lucilius*

IF THERE IS NO GOOD WAY FORWARD, FORGE A BETTER PATH.

Don't follow the herd if it's leading you the wrong way. Elevate your principles and avoid the ordinary and unreflective ways of the masses. Act with integrity, pursue knowledge, and maintain discipline, whether or not it's popular.

STOIC EXERCISE ●

Assess every situation for blind affiliation. Make a checklist: Is this the right way, or the way everyone is going? Is this easy because it's right, or is it easy because it's the path of least resistance?

"SOMEDAY THE MEMORY OF THIS SORROW WILL EVEN BRING DELIGHT."

—Seneca, *Moral Letters to Lucilius*

| DAY **99** | ## TODAY'S STOIC READING
Moral Letters to Lucilius, 78.15
—SENECA |

MISFORTUNE YIELDS FRUIT.

Past and future suffering are undeniable, but you have the power to adapt. Consider how your hardships, losses, and disappointments have contributed to your development. Find strength in adversity, build bonds with loved ones, and accept the value of unexpected choices laid out in front of you.

STOIC EXERCISE ●

Do Hard Things: Write a forgiveness letter. Even if you don't send it, use it to turn over the thoughts and feelings associated with the person or the moment in time. Find a way to let go without bitterness.

"I AM ENDEAVORING
TO LIVE EVERY DAY
AS IF IT WERE A
COMPLETE LIFE. I DO
NOT INDEED SNATCH IT
UP AS IF IT WERE MY
LAST; I DO REGARD IT,
HOWEVER, AS IF IT
MIGHT EVEN
BE MY LAST."

—Seneca, *Moral Letters to Lucilius*

LIVE FULLY EACH DAY.

You don't need to throw caution to the wind or live recklessly. Living fully means acting with contentment and intention. Each day is a promise you make to yourself, and when the sun goes down, peace is yours for the taking.

STOIC EXERCISE ●

Speak to a mentor or someone from an older generation whom you admire. Ask them about their values, memories, and life's accomplishments. Find the threads of golden wisdom in what they have to say and write them down. Refer back to them and discover how they align with or inform your own values.

MY STOIC PRINCIPLES

Jot down what makes these pillars vital to you.

COURAGE

_____

_____

_____

_____

_____

TEMPERANCE

_____

_____

_____

_____

_____

JUSTICE

WISDOM

ABOUT THE AUTHOR

Bryan Sena is a small business consultant with a
background in philosophy. An avid outdoorsman,
Bryan's principles of Stoicism are heavily influenced by nature.
He lives in Bozeman, Montana, with his family.